OFFICIAL SQA PAST PAPERS WITH ANSWERS

STANDARD GRADE | GENERAL

MATHEMATICS
2007-2011

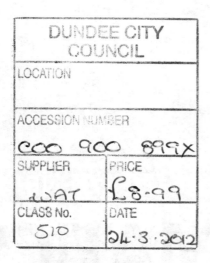
Publisher's Note

We are delighted to bring you the 2011 Past Papers and you will see that we have changed the format from previous editions. As part of our environmental awareness strategy, we have attempted to make these new editions as sustainable as possible.

To do this, we have printed on white paper and bound the answer sections into the book. This not only allows us to use significantly less paper but we are also, for the first time, able to source all the materials from sustainable sources.

We hope you like the new editions and by purchasing this product, you are not only supporting an independent Scottish publishing company but you are also, in the International Year of Forests, not contributing to the destruction of the world's forests.

Thank you for your support and please see the following websites for more information to support the above statement –

www.fsc-uk.org

www.loveforests.com

First exam published in 2007.
Published by Bright Red Publishing Ltd, 6 Stafford Street, Edinburgh EH3 7AU
tel: 0131 220 5804 fax: 0131 220 6710 info@brightredpublishing.co.uk www.brightredpublishing.co.uk

ISBN 978-1-84948-176-2

A CIP Catalogue record for this book is available from the British Library.

Bright Red Publishing is grateful to the copyright holders, as credited on the final page of the Question Section, for permission to use their material. Every effort has been made to trace the copyright holders and to obtain their permission for the use of copyright material. Bright Red Publishing will be happy to receive information allowing us to rectify any error or omission in future editions.

STANDARD GRADE | GENERAL
2007

[BLANK PAGE]

FOR OFFICIAL USE

G

	KU	RE
Total marks		

2500/403

NATIONAL
QUALIFICATIONS
2007

THURSDAY, 3 MAY
10.40 AM – 11.15 AM

MATHEMATICS
STANDARD GRADE
General Level
Paper 1
Non-calculator

Fill in these boxes and read what is printed below.

Full name of centre

Town

Forename(s)

Surname

Date of birth

Day	Month	Year		Scottish candidate number								Number of seat

1 **You may not use a calculator.**

2 Answer as many questions as you can.

3 Write your working and answers in the spaces provided. Additional space is provided at the end of this question-answer book for use if required. If you use this space, write clearly the number of the question involved.

4 Full credit will be given only where the solution contains appropriate working.

5 Before leaving the examination room you must give this book to the invigilator. If you do not you may lose all the marks for this paper.

SCOTTISH
QUALIFICATIONS
AUTHORITY

©

FORMULAE LIST

Circumference of a circle: $C = \pi d$

Area of a circle: $A = \pi r^2$

Curved surface area of a cylinder: $A = 2\pi rh$

Volume of a cylinder: $V = \pi r^2 h$

Volume of a triangular prism: $V = Ah$

Theorem of Pythagoras:

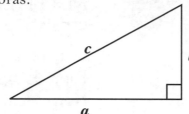

$$a^2 + b^2 = c^2$$

Trigonometric ratios
in a right angled
triangle:

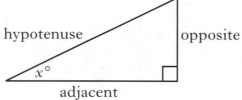

$$\tan x^\circ = \frac{\text{opposite}}{\text{adjacent}}$$

$$\sin x^\circ = \frac{\text{opposite}}{\text{hypotenuse}}$$

$$\cos x^\circ = \frac{\text{adjacent}}{\text{hypotenuse}}$$

Gradient:

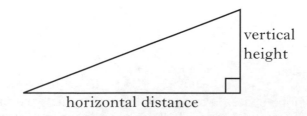

$$\text{Gradient} = \frac{\text{vertical height}}{\text{horizontal distance}}$$

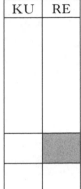

Marks

1. Carry out the following calculations.

(a) $4 \cdot 27 - 1 \cdot 832$

1

(b) $6 \cdot 53 \times 40$

1

(c) $372 \div 8$

1

(d) $5 \times 4\frac{1}{3}$

2

2. A particle is radioactive for $2 \cdot 3 \times 10^{-4}$ seconds.

Write this number in full.

2

Marks | KU | RE

3. Zoe is a member of a gym.

The gym offers the following exercise sessions.

Exercise	Session Time
Weights	15 minutes
Dance	40 minutes
Running	20 minutes
Cycling	30 minutes
Swimming	45 minutes

Zoe is advised to choose **three** different exercises.

She wants to exercise for a **minimum of 90 minutes**.

One possible combination of three different exercises is shown in the table below.

Complete the table to show all the possible combinations of three different exercises Zoe can choose.

Weights	Dance	Running	Cycling	Swimming	Total Time (minutes)
		✓	✓	✓	95 minutes

3

DO NOT
WRITE IN
THIS
MARGIN

Marks | KU | RE

4. Complete this shape so that it has quarter-turn symmetry about O.

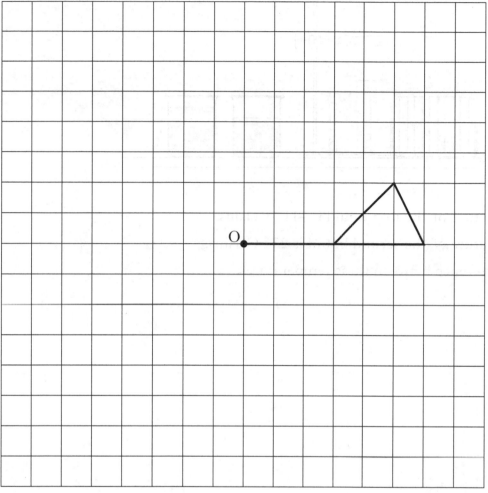

3

[Turn over

Marks | KU | RE

5. In an experiment Rashid measures the temperature of two liquids.

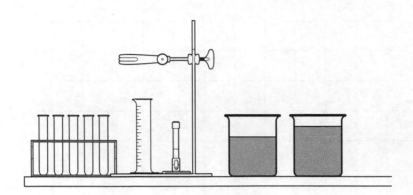

The temperature of the first liquid is −11° Celsius.

The temperature of the second liquid is 23° Celsius.

Find the difference between these temperatures.

34°C

2

Marks | KU | RE

6. A children's play area is to be fenced.

The fence is made in sections using lengths of wood, as shown below.

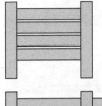

1 section

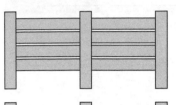

2 sections

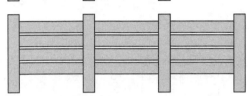

3 sections

(*a*) Complete the table below.

Number of sections (*s*)	1	2	3	4	5		12
Number of lengths of wood (*w*)	6	11	16	21	26		61

2

(*b*) Write down a formula for calculating the number of lengths of wood (*w*), when you know the number of sections (*s*).

$$5S + 1 = W$$

2

(*c*) A fence has been made from 81 lengths of wood.

How many sections are in this fence?

You must show your working.

$$81 - 1 = 80$$
$$80 \div 5 = 16$$

2

Marks | KU | RE

7. The table below shows the marks scored by pupils in French and Italian exams.

Pupil	A	B	C	D	E	F	G	H
French Mark	15	23	50	38	40	42	70	82
Italian Mark	28	31	62	54	45	55	85	95

(a) Using these marks, draw a scattergraph.

2

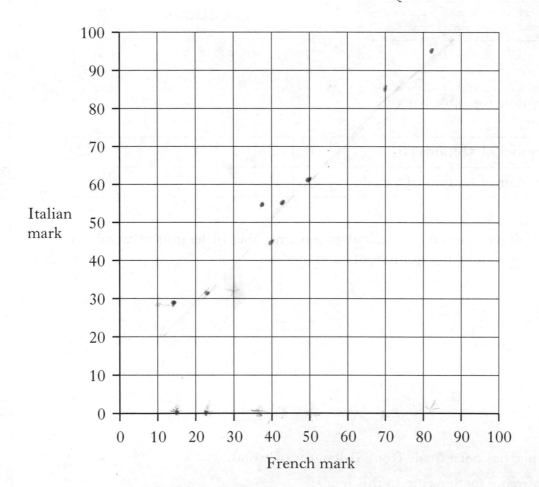

(b) Draw a best-fitting line on the graph.

1

Marks   KU   RE

7. (continued)

(*c*) A pupil who scored 65 in his French exam was absent from the Italian exam.

Use your best-fitting line to estimate this pupil's Italian mark.

1

8. Pamela sees a bracelet costing £65 in a jeweller's window.

The jeweller offers Pamela a 5% discount.

Pamela decides to buy the bracelet.

How much does she pay?

1% of £65 = 65p

65 × 5 = 3.25   discount

65 − 3.25 = 61.75

3

DO NOT WRITE IN THIS MARGIN

Marks KU RE

9. Craig works in the school office.

Shown below is his order for 25 boxes of folders.

Office Supplies	
Blue Folders	7 boxes
Green Folders	11 boxes
Pink Folders	3 boxes
Yellow Folders	4 boxes
Total	**25 boxes**

His order has arrived in identical boxes but they are not labelled.

(*a*) What is the probability that the first box Craig opens contains pink folders?

$\frac{3}{25}$ ✓

1

(*b*) The first box Craig opens contains green folders.

What is the probability that the next box he opens contains blue folders?

$\frac{7}{24}$ ✓

2

10. There are 720 pupils in Laggan High School.

The ratio of boys to girls in the school is 5 : 4.

How many girls are in the school?

$720 \div 9 = 80$

$4 \times 80 = 320$ ✓

3

[END OF QUESTION PAPER]

ADDITIONAL SPACE FOR ANSWERS

FOR OFFICIAL USE

G

	KU	RE
Total marks		

2500/404

NATIONAL
QUALIFICATIONS
2007

THURSDAY, 3 MAY
11.35 AM – 12.30 PM

MATHEMATICS
STANDARD GRADE
General Level
Paper 2

Fill in these boxes and read what is printed below.

Full name of centre

Town

Forename(s)

Surname

Date of birth

Day Month Year   Scottish candidate number   Number of seat

1 **You may use a calculator.**

2 Answer as many questions as you can.

3 Write your working and answers in the spaces provided. Additional space is provided at the end of this question-answer book for use if required. If you use this space, write clearly the number of the question involved.

4 Full credit will be given only where the solution contains appropriate working.

5 Before leaving the examination room you must give this book to the invigilator. If you do not you may lose all the marks for this paper.

SCOTTISH
QUALIFICATIONS
AUTHORITY

FORMULAE LIST

Circumference of a circle:　　　　$C = \pi d$

Area of a circle:　　　　　　　　$A = \pi r^2$

Curved surface area of a cylinder:　$A = 2\pi rh$

Volume of a cylinder:　　　　　　$V = \pi r^2 h$

Volume of a triangular prism:　　　$V = Ah$

Theorem of Pythagoras:

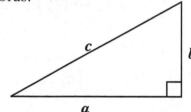

$$a^2 + b^2 = c^2$$

Trigonometric ratios
in a right angled
triangle:

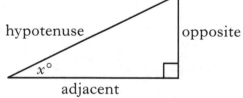

$$\tan x° = \frac{\text{opposite}}{\text{adjacent}}$$

$$\sin x° = \frac{\text{opposite}}{\text{hypotenuse}}$$

$$\cos x° = \frac{\text{adjacent}}{\text{hypotenuse}}$$

Gradient:

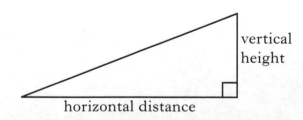

$$\text{Gradient} = \frac{\text{vertical height}}{\text{horizontal distance}}$$

Marks | KU | RE

1. A Sprinter train travels at an average speed of 144 kilometres per hour.

The train takes 1 hour 15 minutes to travel between Dingwall and Aberdeen.

Calculate the distance between Dingwall and Aberdeen.

$$\frac{144}{60}=$$

144 kph

$$15 = \frac{1}{4} \text{ hour}$$

$$144 \div 4 = 36$$

$$36 \times 5 = 180$$

2

[Turn over

Marks | KU | RE

2. Mr McGill is a bricklayer.

He builds a wall using 7500 bricks:

- each brick costs 23 pence
- a charge of £200 is made for every 500 bricks he lays.

What is the **total** cost of building the wall?

$7500 \times 23 = 7223$

$7223 \div 100 = £72.23$

$7500 \div 500 =$

$7500 \div 500 = 15$

$15 \times 200 = £3000$

£3000
£72.23
2.23

$3000 + 72.23 = 3072.23$

3

Marks | KU | RE

3.

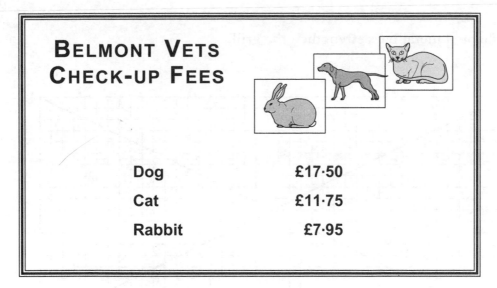

BELMONT VETS CHECK-UP FEES

Dog	**£17·50**
Cat	**£11·75**
Rabbit	**£7·95**

The Wilson family owns two dogs and a cat.

Last year each dog had two check-ups at Belmont Vets.

The family cat also had check-ups last year.

The Wilson's total check-up fees for the two dogs and the cat were £105·25.

How often did the cat have a check-up?

£17.50 × 4 = £70

£105.25 ~~×~~ −£70 = £35.25

£35.25 ÷ 11.75 = 3

Cat went 3 times to the vet.

4

[Turn over

Marks | KU | RE

4. A rectangular metal grill for a window is shown below.

Two diagonal metal bars strengthen the grill.

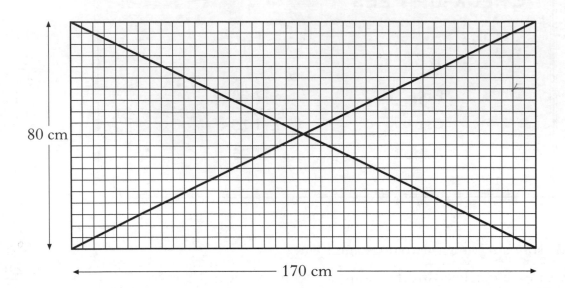

80 cm

170 cm

Find the length of one of the metal bars.

Round your answer to the nearest centimetre.

Do not use a scale drawing.

$170^2 - 80^2 = 22,600$

$\sqrt{22500}$

$\sqrt{25}$ $\sqrt{22500} = 150$

1 bar = 150 cm

4

Marks | KU | RE

5. (*a*) Simplify

$$2(3x + 7) + 4(3 - x).$$

$6x + 14 + 12 - 4x$

$2x + 26$

3

(*b*) Solve the inequality

$$4a - 3 \geq 21.$$

$4a \geq 21 - 3$

$4a \geq 78$

2

[Turn over

6. DEFG is a kite:

- angle DEG = 35°
- EF = 14 centimetres.

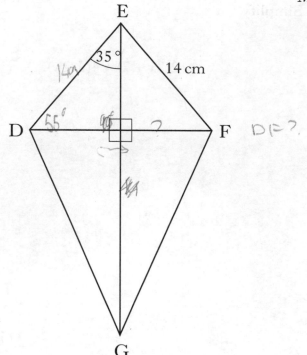

Calculate the length of DF.

4

Marks | KU | RE

7. A supermarket has a canopy over its entrance.

The edge of the canopy has 6 semicircles as shown below.

← 4 m →

Each semicircle has a diameter of 4 metres.

(a) Find the length of the curved edge of **one of the semicircles**.

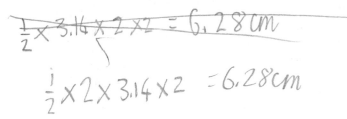

$\frac{1}{2} \times 3.14 \times 2 \times 2 = 6.28\,cm$

$\frac{1}{2} \times 2 \times 3.14 \times 2 = 6.28\,cm$

2

(b) Tony attaches fairy lights to the edge of the canopy.

He has 40 metres of fairy lights.

Is this enough for the whole canopy?

Give a reason for your answer.

$6.28 \times 6 = 37.68$

Yes tony will have enough fairy lights
to light the whole canopy

2

Marks | KU | RE

8.

Platinum
Saver Account

6·3% interest per annum

Sally invests £4200 in the Platinum Saver Account which pays 6·3% interest per annum.

How much simple interest will she receive after 10 months?

$$4200 \times \frac{106.3}{100} = 4464.6$$

$4464.6 \div 12 = 372.05$

$372.05 \times 10 = 3720.5$

$4464.6 -$

$4464.6 - 4200 = 264.6$

$264.6 \div 12 = 22.05$

$22.05 \times 10 = £220.5$

3

Marks   KU   RE

9. In the diagram:

  • O is the centre of the circle
  • AC is a diameter
  • B is a point on the circumference
  • angle BAC = 43°.

Calculate the size of shaded angle BOC.

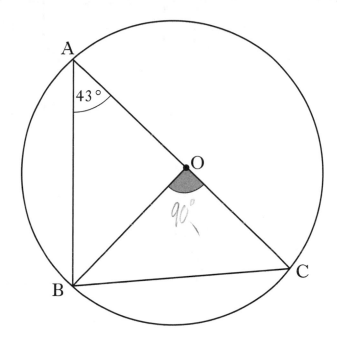

3

Marks | KU | RE

10. The end face of a grain hopper is shown in the diagram.

(a) Calculate the area of the end face.

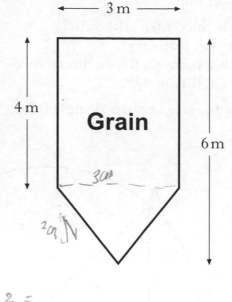

$1.5 \text{ cm} \times 2 =$

$\frac{1}{2} b \times h$

$\frac{1}{2} \times 3 \times 2 = 3 \text{ sq. cm.}$

Area of end face
$= (4 \times 3) + \frac{1}{2} \times 3 \times 2 =$
$= 12 + 3 = 15 \text{ sq. m.}$

3

(b) The grain hopper is in the shape of a prism with a length of 3·5 metres.

Find the volume of the hopper.

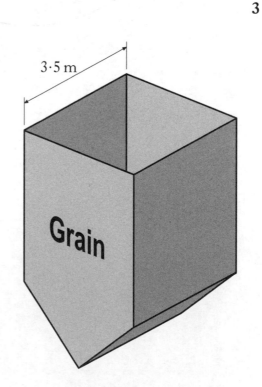

cross section $= 3 + 12 = 15 \text{ m}^2$

$15 \times 3.5 = 52.5 \text{ cu.m.}$

$= 52.5 \text{ m}^3$

2

Marks KU RE

11. The diagram below shows the design for a house window.

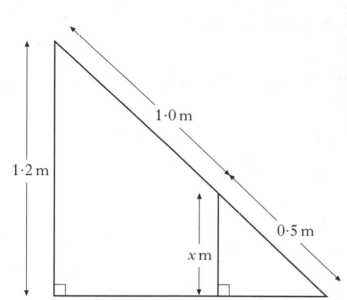

Find the value of x.

3

[Turn over for Question 12 on *Page fourteen*

Marks | KU | RE

12. The burning time, t minutes, of a candle varies directly as its height, h millimetres.

A candle with a height of 75 millimetres burns for 180 minutes.

(a) What is the burning time of a 40 millimetre candle?

$180 \div 75 = 2.4$

$40 \times 2.4 = 168$

$40 \times 2.4 = 96$

3

(b) A candle burns for $2\frac{1}{2}$ hours.

What is the height of this candle?

3

[END OF QUESTION PAPER]

ADDITIONAL SPACE FOR ANSWERS

ADDITIONAL SPACE FOR ANSWERS

STANDARD GRADE | GENERAL

2008

[BLANK PAGE]

FOR OFFICIAL USE

G

KU   RE

Total marks

2500/403

NATIONAL
QUALIFICATIONS
2008

THURSDAY, 8 MAY
10.40 AM – 11.15 AM

MATHEMATICS
STANDARD GRADE
General Level
Paper 1
Non-calculator

Fill in these boxes and read what is printed below.

Full name of centre

Town

Forename(s)

Surname

Date of birth

Day Month Year   Scottish candidate number   Number of seat

1 **You may not use a calculator.**

2 Answer as many questions as you can.

3 Write your working and answers in the spaces provided. Additional space is provided at the end of this question-answer book for use if required. If you use this space, write clearly the number of the question involved.

4 Full credit will be given only where the solution contains appropriate working.

5 Before leaving the examination room you must give this book to the invigilator. If you do not you may lose all the marks for this paper.

FORMULAE LIST

Circumference of a circle: $C = \pi d$

Area of a circle: $A = \pi r^2$

Curved surface area of a cylinder: $A = 2\pi rh$

Volume of a cylinder: $V = \pi r^2 h$

Volume of a triangular prism: $V = Ah$

Theorem of Pythagoras:

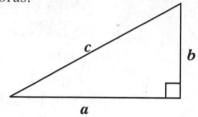

$$a^2 + b^2 = c^2$$

Trigonometric ratios
in a right angled
triangle:

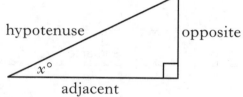

$$\tan x° = \frac{\text{opposite}}{\text{adjacent}}$$

$$\sin x° = \frac{\text{opposite}}{\text{hypotenuse}}$$

$$\cos x° = \frac{\text{adjacent}}{\text{hypotenuse}}$$

Gradient:

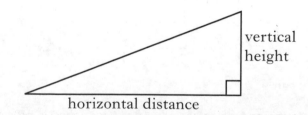

$$\textbf{Gradient} = \frac{\text{vertical height}}{\text{horizontal distance}}$$

Marks | KU | RE

1. Carry out the following calculations.

(*a*) $12 \cdot 76 - 3 \cdot 18 + 4 \cdot 59$

1

(*b*) $6 \cdot 39 \times 9$

1

(*c*) $8 \cdot 74 \div 200$

1

(*d*) $\frac{5}{6}$ of 420

2

[Turn over

Marks | KU | RE

2. In the "Fame Show", the percentage of telephone votes cast for each act is shown below.

Plastik Money	23%
Brian Martins	35%
Starshine	30%
Carrie Gordon	12%

Altogether 15 000 000 votes were cast.

How many votes did Starshine receive?

3

Marks | KU | RE

3. AB and BC are two sides of a kite ABCD.

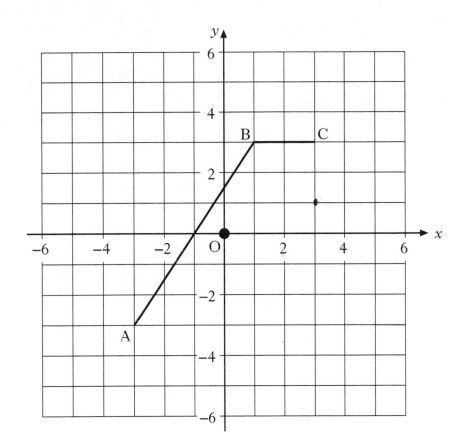

(a) Plot point D to complete kite ABCD.   1

(b) Reflect kite ABCD in the **y-axis**.

3

Marks | KU | RE

4. Europe is the world's second smallest continent.

Its area is approximately 10 400 000 square kilometres.

Write this number in scientific notation.

2

Marks | KU | RE

5. Samantha is playing the computer game "Castle Challenge".

To enter the castle she needs the correct four digit code.

The computer gives her some clues:

• only digits 1 to 9 can be used
• each digit is greater than the one before
• the sum of all four digits is 14.

(*a*) The first code Samantha found was 1, 3, 4, 6.

Use the clues to list all the possible codes in the table below.

1	3	4	6

3

(*b*) The computer gives Samantha another clue.

• three of the digits in the code are prime numbers

What is the four digit code Samantha needs to enter the castle?

1

[Turn over

DO NOT WRITE IN THIS MARGIN

Marks KU RE

6.

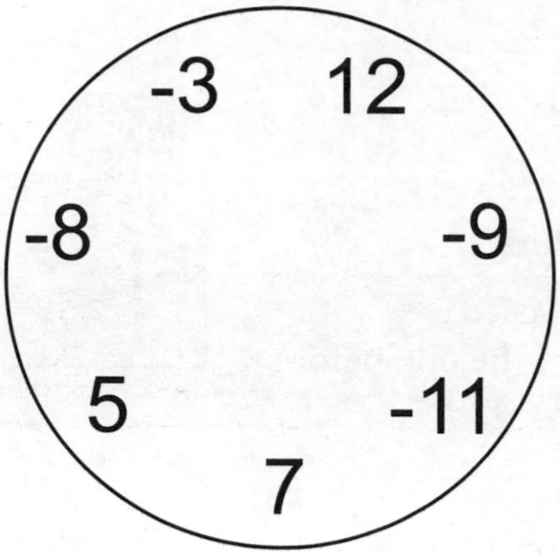

The circle above contains seven numbers.

Find the three numbers from the circle which add up to -10.

You must show your working. 3

Marks | KU | RE

7. The cost of sending a letter depends on the size of the letter and the weight of the letter.

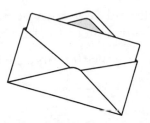

Format	Weight	Cost	
		1st Class Mail	2nd Class Mail
Letter	0–100 g	34p	24p
Large Letter	0–100 g	48p	40p
	101–250 g	70p	60p
	251–500 g	98p	83p
	501–750 g	142p	120p

Claire sends a letter weighing 50 g by 2nd class mail.

She also sends a large letter weighing 375 g by 1st class mail.

Use the table above to calculate the total cost.

3

[Turn over

Marks   KU   RE

8. Four girls and two boys decide to organise a tennis tournament for themselves.

Each name is written on a plastic token and put in a bag.

(*a*) What is the probability that the first token drawn from the bag has a girl's name on it?

1

(*b*) The first token drawn from the bag has a girl's name on it.

This token is **not** returned to the bag.

What is the probability that the next token drawn from the bag has a boy's name on it?

2

Marks | KU | RE

9.

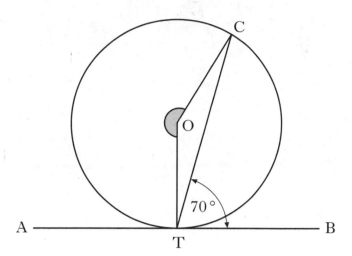

In the diagram above:

- O is the centre of the circle
- AB is a tangent to the circle at T
- angle BTC = 70°.

Calculate the size of the shaded angle TOC.

3

[END OF QUESTION PAPER]

ADDITIONAL SPACE FOR ANSWERS

FOR OFFICIAL USE

G

	KU	RE
Total marks		

2500/404

NATIONAL
QUALIFICATIONS
2008

THURSDAY, 8 MAY
11.35 AM – 12.30 PM

MATHEMATICS
STANDARD GRADE
General Level
Paper 2

Fill in these boxes and read what is printed below.

Full name of centre

Town

Forename(s)

Surname

Date of birth

Day Month Year   Scottish candidate number   Number of seat

1 **You may use a calculator.**

2 Answer as many questions as you can.

3 Write your working and answers in the spaces provided. Additional space is provided at the end of this question-answer book for use if required. If you use this space, write clearly the number of the question involved.

4 Full credit will be given only where the solution contains appropriate working.

5 Before leaving the examination room you must give this book to the invigilator. If you do not you may lose all the marks for this paper.

FORMULAE LIST

Circumference of a circle: $\qquad$ $C = \pi d$

Area of a circle: $\qquad$ $A = \pi r^2$

Curved surface area of a cylinder: $\qquad$ $A = 2\pi rh$

Volume of a cylinder: $\qquad$ $V = \pi r^2 h$

Volume of a triangular prism: $\qquad$ $V = Ah$

Theorem of Pythagoras:

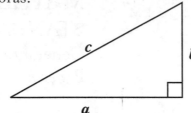

$$a^2 + b^2 = c^2$$

Trigonometric ratios
in a right angled
triangle:

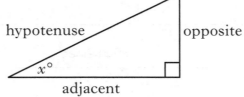

$$\tan x^\circ = \frac{\text{opposite}}{\text{adjacent}}$$

$$\sin x^\circ = \frac{\text{opposite}}{\text{hypotenuse}}$$

$$\cos x^\circ = \frac{\text{adjacent}}{\text{hypotenuse}}$$

Gradient:

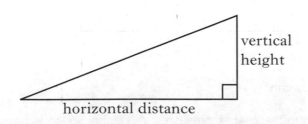

$$\text{Gradient} = \frac{\text{vertical height}}{\text{horizontal distance}}$$

DO NOT
WRITE IN
THIS
MARGIN

Marks | KU | RE

1. Corrina has a part time job in a local pottery.

She paints designs on coffee mugs.

Her basic rate of pay is £6·25 per hour.

She also gets paid an extra 22 pence for every mug she paints.

Last week Corrina worked 15 hours and painted 40 mugs.

How much was she paid?

3

[Turn over

DO NOT
WRITE IN
THIS
MARGIN

Marks | KU | RE

2. Charlie's new car has an on-board computer.

At the end of a journey the car's computer displays the information below.

Journey information

distance **157.5 miles**

average speed **45 miles/hour**

Use the information above to calculate the time he has taken for his journey.

Give your answer in hours and minutes.

4

Marks | KU | RE

3.

Ben needs 550 grams of flour to bake two small loaves of bread.

(*a*) How many **kilograms** of flour will he need for thirteen small loaves?

1 = loaf of bread

$550 \div 2 = 275$

$275 = 1k$

$13 \times 275 = 3575\,g$

$3575 \div 1000 = 3.575\,kg$

2

Ben buys his flour in 1·5 kilogram bags.

(*b*) How many bags of flour will he need to bake the thirteen small loaves?

3

1

[Turn over

Marks KU RE

4. Mhairi makes necklaces in M-shapes using silver bars.

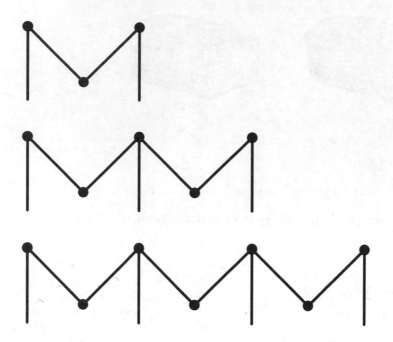

(*a*) Complete the table below.

Number of M-shapes (*m*)	1	2	3	4		15
Number of bars (*b*)	4	7	10	13		46

2

$n=1 \times 2$

(*b*) Write down a formula for calculating the number of bars (*b*) when you know the number of M-shapes (*m*).

2

(*c*) Mhairi has 76 silver bars.

How many M-shapes can she make?

2

5. Lewis is designing a bird box for his garden.

The dimensions for the side of the box are shown in the diagram below.

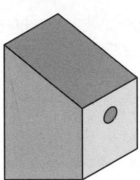

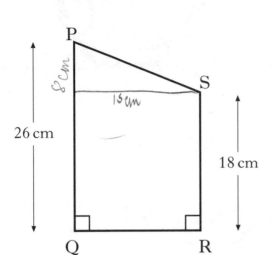

Calculate the length of side PS.

Do not use a scale drawing.

$\sqrt{}$ = $15 \times 15 = 225$
$8 \times 8 = 64$

= $225 + 64 = 289$

$\sqrt{289}$ = 17

$PS = 17cm$

4

[Turn over

Marks | KU | RE

6. Gordon buys an antique teapot for £95.

He sells it on an Internet auction site for £133.

Calculate his percentage profit.

$\frac{38}{95} \times 100 = 140$

$\frac{133}{95} \times 100$

$= 40\%$

3

Marks | KU | RE

7. A piece of glass from a stained glass window is shown below.

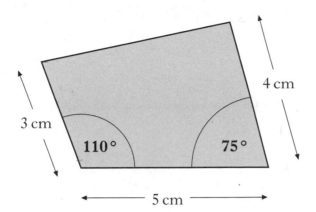

A larger piece of glass, the same shape, is to be made using a scale of 2:1.

Make an accurate drawing of the larger piece of glass.

3

[Turn over

DO NOT
WRITE IN
THIS
MARGIN

Marks KU RE

8. (*a*) Solve algebraically

$$7t - 3 = t + 45.$$

$7t - t = 45 + 3$

$6t = 48$

$t = 8$

3

(*b*) Factorise fully

$$20x - 12y.$$

$4(5x - 3y)$

20

5×4

$5 \times 2 \times 2$

2

Marks | KU | RE

9. Ian is making a sign for Capaldi's Ice Cream Parlour.

The sign will have two equal straight edges and a semi-circular edge.

Each straight edge is 2·25 metres long and the radius of the semi-circle is 0·9 metres.

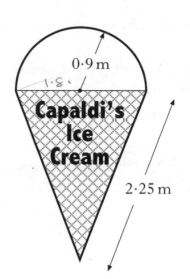

0·9 m

Capaldi's Ice Cream

2·25 m

Calculate the perimeter of the sign.

$2 \times \frac{3.14}{4} \times 3.16$

$2 \times 3.14 \times 1.8$

ⓐ of Semi ☉ $= \frac{1}{2} \times 2 \times \pi \times \cdot 9$

$= 3.41 \times \cdot 9$

$= 3.69$

$= 2.8269 +$

4

[Turn over

Marks KU RE

10. Natalie wanted to know the average number of hours cars were parked in a car park.

She did a survey of 100 cars which were parked in the car park on a particular day.

Her results are shown below.

Parking time (hours)	Frequency	Parking time × frequency
1	28	
2	22	
3	10	
4	15	
5	11	
6	5	
7	9	
	Total = 100	Total =

Complete the above table and find the mean parking time per car.

3

Marks   KU   RE

11. Circular tops for yoghurt cartons are cut from a strip of metal foil as shown below.

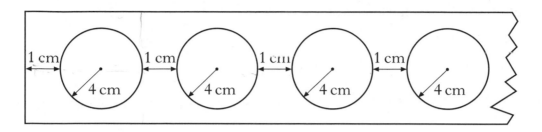

The radius of each top is 4 centimetres.

The gap between each top is 1 centimetre.

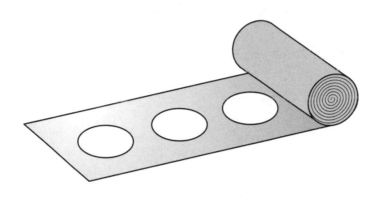

How many tops can be cut from a strip of foil 7 metres long?

4

Page thirteen   **[Turn over**

Marks   KU   RE

12. A boat elevator is used to take a boat from the lower canal to the upper canal.

The boat elevator is in the shape of a triangle.

The length of the hypotenuse is 109 metres.

The height of the triangle is 45 metres.

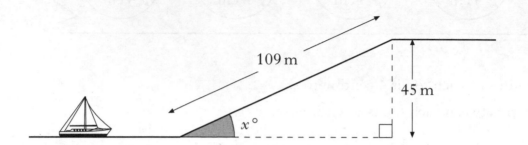

Calculate the size of the shaded angle $x°$.

$$\frac{45}{109}$$

3

Marks | KU | RE

13. A wheelie bin is in the shape of a cuboid.

The dimensions of the bin are:

- length 70 centimetres
- breadth 60 centimetres
- height 95 centimetres.

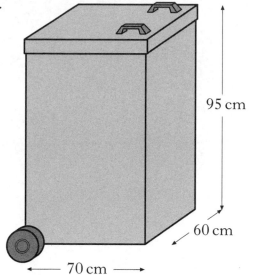

95 cm

60 cm

70 cm

(a) Calculate the volume of the bin.

2

(b) The council is considering a new design of wheelie bin.

The new bin will have the same volume as the old one.

The base of the new bin is to be a square of side 55 centimetres.

Calculate the height of the new wheelie bin.

3

[END OF QUESTION PAPER]

ADDITIONAL SPACE FOR ANSWERS

STANDARD GRADE | GENERAL

2009

[BLANK PAGE]

G

FOR OFFICIAL USE

	KU	RE
Total marks		

2500/403

NATIONAL QUALIFICATIONS 2009	WEDNESDAY, 6 MAY 10.40 AM – 11.15 AM	**MATHEMATICS** STANDARD GRADE General Level Paper 1 Non-calculator

Fill in these boxes and read what is printed below.

Full name of centre

Town

Forename(s)

Surname

Date of birth

Day Month Year

Scottish candidate number

Number of seat

1 **You may <u>not</u> use a calculator.**

2 Answer as many questions as you can.

3 Write your working and answers in the spaces provided. Additional space is provided at the end of this question-answer book for use if required. If you use this space, write clearly the number of the question involved.

4 Full credit will be given only where the solution contains appropriate working.

5 Before leaving the examination room you must give this book to the invigilator. If you do not you may lose all the marks for this paper.

FORMULAE LIST

Circumference of a circle: $C = \pi d$

Area of a circle: $A = \pi r^2$

Curved surface area of a cylinder: $A = 2\pi rh$

Volume of a cylinder: $V = \pi r^2 h$

Volume of a triangular prism: $V = Ah$

Theorem of Pythagoras:

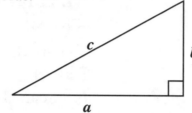

$$a^2 + b^2 = c^2$$

Trigonometric ratios
in a right angled
triangle:

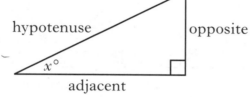

$$\tan x° = \frac{\text{opposite}}{\text{adjacent}}$$

$$\sin x° = \frac{\text{opposite}}{\text{hypotenuse}}$$

$$\cos x° = \frac{\text{adjacent}}{\text{hypotenuse}}$$

Gradient:

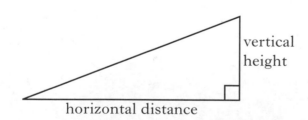

$$\text{Gradient} = \frac{\text{vertical height}}{\text{horizontal distance}}$$

DO NOT WRITE IN THIS MARGIN

Marks | KU | RE

1. Carry out the following calculations.

(a) $17 \cdot 3 - 14 \cdot 86$

1

(b) 23×6000

1

(c) $256 \cdot 9 \div 7$

1

(d) 80% of 54

2

[Turn over

Marks

2. An old unit of measurement called a fluid ounce is equal to 0·0296 litres.

Write 0·0296 in scientific notation.

2

DO NOT
WRITE IN
THIS
MARGIN

Marks | KU | RE

3. Samira is designing a chain belt.

Each section of the belt is made from metal rings as shown below.

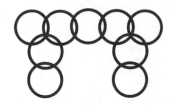

1 section, 4 rings

2 sections, 9 rings

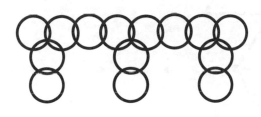

3 sections

(a) Complete the table below.

Number of sections (s)	1	2	3	4	5		11
Number of metal rings (r)	4	9					

2

(b) Write down a formula for calculating the number of rings (r), when you know the number of sections (s).

2

(c) Samira uses 79 rings to make her belt.

How many sections does her belt have?

2

4. A floor is to be tiled using tiles shaped like this.

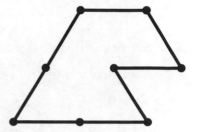

Here is part of the tiling.

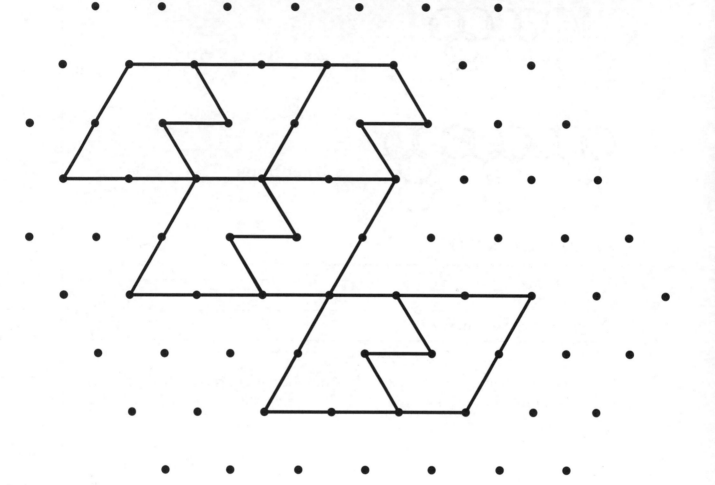

Draw **four** more tiles to continue the tiling.

3

Marks

KU | RE

5. (a) On the grid below, plot the points A(2, 6), B(8, 2) and C(6, –1).

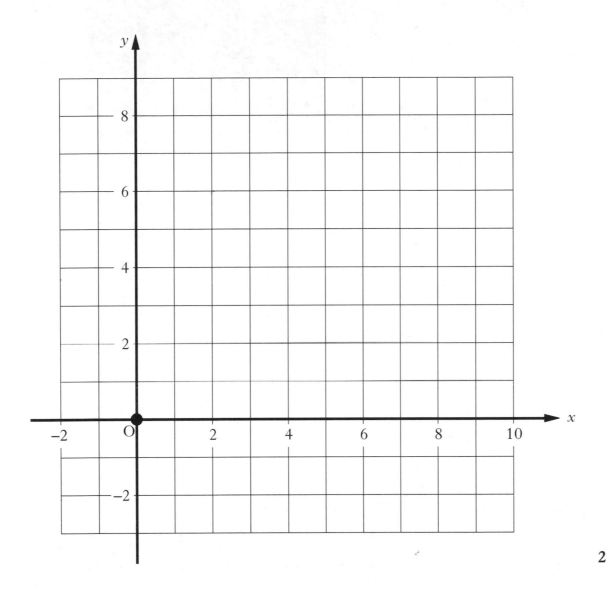

2

(b) Plot a fourth point D so that ABCD is a rectangle.   1

(c) On the grid, show the point where the diagonals of the rectangle intersect.

Write down the coordinates of this point.

2

Marks   KU   RE

6. In July the average temperature in Anchorage, Alaska is 9 °C.

By January the average temperature has fallen by 26 °C.

What is the average temperature in Anchorage in January?

2

Marks | KU | RE

7. Joe is making a fruit pudding on Scottish Master Chef.

In the fruit pudding recipe the ratio of raspberries to blackberries is 5:1.

Joe's fruit pudding must contain a **total** of 240 grams of fruit.

Calculate the weight of raspberries in his pudding.

3

[Turn over

Marks KU RE

8. Each pupil in a science class is growing a plant.

A few weeks later the height of each plant is measured.

The heights in centimetres are shown below.

| 6·3 | 5·4 | 5·8 | 7·0 | 6·2 | 7·6 | 8·3 | 8·4 | 5·3 | 8·8 |
| 8·5 | 5·6 | 6·8 | 6·5 | 6·1 | 6·7 | 7·4 | 7·6 | 5·3 | |

(*a*) Display these results in an ordered stem and leaf diagram.

3

(*b*) Find the median height.

1

Marks   KU   RE

9.   In the diagram below:

- triangle ABD is isosceles with AB = AD
- angle DAB = 34°
- angle ABC = 90°
- angle BCD = 20°.

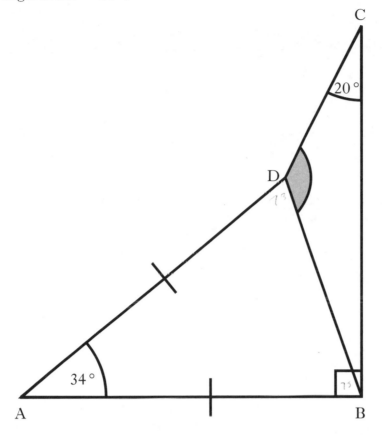

Calculate the size of the shaded angle BDC.

3

[END OF QUESTION PAPER]

ADDITIONAL SPACE FOR ANSWERS

FOR OFFICIAL USE

G

	KU	RE
Total marks		

2500/404

NATIONAL QUALIFICATIONS 2009

WEDNESDAY, 6 MAY 11.35 AM – 12.30 PM

MATHEMATICS
STANDARD GRADE
General Level
Paper 2

Fill in these boxes and read what is printed below.

Full name of centre

Town

Forename(s)

Surname

Date of birth

Day Month Year   Scottish candidate number   Number of seat

1 **You may use a calculator.**

2 Answer as many questions as you can.

3 Write your working and answers in the spaces provided. Additional space is provided at the end of this question-answer book for use if required. If you use this space, write clearly the number of the question involved.

4 Full credit will be given only where the solution contains appropriate working.

5 Before leaving the examination room you must give this book to the invigilator. If you do not you may lose all the marks for this paper.

FORMULAE LIST

Circumference of a circle: $C = \pi d$

Area of a circle: $A = \pi r^2$

Curved surface area of a cylinder: $A = 2\pi rh$

Volume of a cylinder: $V = \pi r^2 h$

Volume of a triangular prism: $V = Ah$

Theorem of Pythagoras:

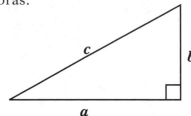

$$a^2 + b^2 = c^2$$

Trigonometric ratios
in a right angled
triangle:

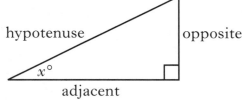

$$\tan x° = \frac{\text{opposite}}{\text{adjacent}}$$

$$\sin x° = \frac{\text{opposite}}{\text{hypotenuse}}$$

$$\cos x° = \frac{\text{adjacent}}{\text{hypotenuse}}$$

Gradient:

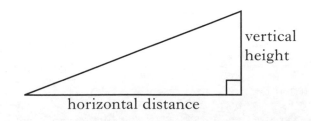

$$\text{Gradient} = \frac{\text{vertical height}}{\text{horizontal distance}}$$

1. Naveen drives from Dumfries to Manchester.

   A 28 mile part of his journey is affected by roadworks.

   It takes him 40 minutes to drive this part of his journey.

   Calculate his average speed for this part of his journey.

   Give your answer in miles per hour.

3

[Turn over

Marks KU RE

2. Helen travels between Glasgow and Edinburgh by train.

   She buys a monthly TravelPass which costs £264·30.

   A daily return ticket would cost £16·90.

   Last month Helen made 19 return journeys.

   How much did she save by buying the TravelPass?

3

Marks

KU	RE

3. A semi-circular window in the school assembly hall is made from three identical panes of glass.

During a recent storm one pane of glass was damaged.

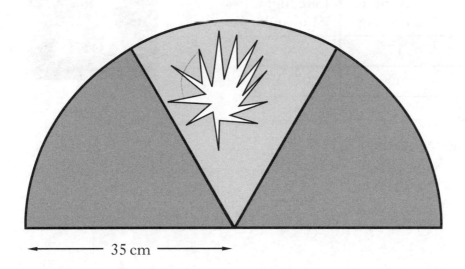

— 35 cm —

The semi-circle has a radius of 35 centimetres.

Calculate the area of the damaged pane of glass.

3

[Turn over

Marks | KU | RF

4. John is going to see a movie.

The movie has an evening and a late night showing.

	Evening showing	Late night showing
Start time	1750	
Finish time	2005	0110

(a) How long does the movie last?

1

(b) When does the late night showing start?

2

Marks | KU | RE

5. (*a*) Factorise

$$6c - 15d.$$

2

(*b*) Simplify

$$5(a + 1) + 2(5 - 2a).$$

3

[Turn over

Marks   KU   RE

6. David is trying to decide which channel mixes to buy for his TV system.

The cost of each is:

- Drama Mix   £7
- Sport Mix   £20
- Movies Mix   £15
- Kids Mix   £12
- Music Mix   £10

He has decided to buy four different mixes.

One possible selection and its cost are shown in the table below.

(a) Complete the table showing all the possible selections and the cost of each.

Selections				Cost
Drama	Sport	Movies	Music	£52

3

(b) David can spend up to £55 for his selection.

Which selection can he **not** buy?

1

Marks

KU | RE

7. Last week Theresa asked 76 students to record how many hours they spent doing homework.

The results are shown below.

Homework hours	Frequency	Homework hours × frequency
1	16	
2	12	
3	18	
4	11	
5	8	
6	6	
7	5	
	Total = 76	Total =

Complete the above table and find the **mean** time spent on homework last week.

Round your answer to 1 decimal place.

4

Marks

8. A steel plate in the shape of an isosceles triangle is used to strengthen a bridge.

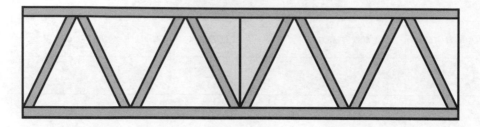

The dimensions of the isosceles triangle are shown below.

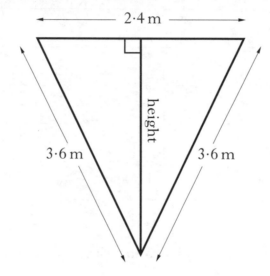

Calculate the height of the steel plate.

Do not use a scale drawing.

4

Marks | KU | RE

9.

Pizza Perfection — free delivery				
	Deep Base		Thin Base	
	9-inch	12-inch	9-inch	12-inch
Margherita	£3·60	£5·00	£3·30	£4·60
Mushroom	£4·25	£5·80	£4·15	£5·50
Pepperoni	£5·00	£6·30	£4·90	£6·00
Vegetarian	£5·05	£6·35	£4·95	£6·05
Hot Spicy	£5·15	£6·45	£5·05	£6·15

Iona and her friends order some pizzas to be delivered.

They order a 9-inch Hot Spicy deep base, a 12-inch Margherita deep base and two 12-inch Vegetarian thin base.

Find the total cost of the order.

3

[Turn over

Marks | KU | RE

10. Susan has £6200 in her Clydeside Bank account.

Clydeside Bank pays interest at 2·5% per annum.

Highland Bank pays interest at 3·7% per annum.

How much more money would Susan get in interest if she moved her £6200 to the Highland Bank for one year?

3

Marks | KU | RE

11. The shaded part of a garden light is triangular.

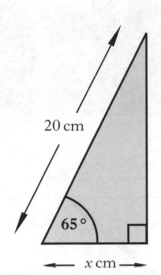

20 cm

65°

← x cm →

- the triangle is right angled
- the sloping edge is 20 centimetres long
- the angle between the base and the sloping edge is 65°.

Calculate the value of x.

3

Marks KU RE

12. The local council is installing a new children's playpark using a rubberised material.

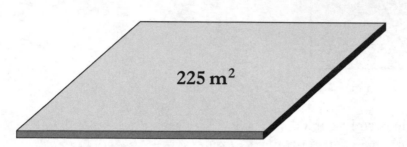

225 m²

The area of the rectangular playpark is 225 square metres.

The new playpark must have a depth of 12 centimetres.

The council has ordered 30 cubic metres of the rubberised material for the playpark.

Will this be enough?

Give a reason for your answer.

3

Marks | KU | RE |

13. An off shore wind farm is on a bearing of 115° and at a distance of 90 kilometres from Eyemouth.

Using a scale of 1 centimetre to represent 10 kilometres, show the position of the wind farm on the diagram below.

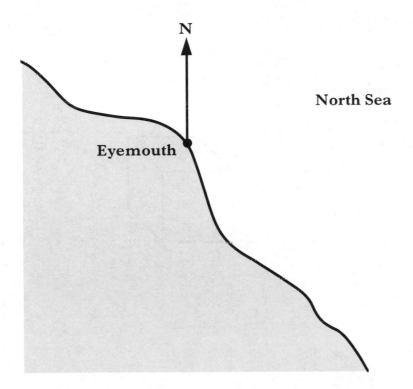

N

North Sea

Eyemouth

3

[Turn over for Question 14 on *Page sixteen*

Marks | KU | RE

14. The diagram below shows the net of a cube.

The total surface area of the cube is 150 square centimetres.

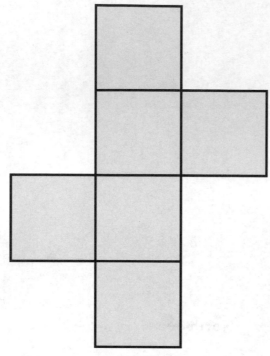

Net of Cube

Calculate the length of the side of the cube.

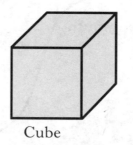

Cube

3

[END OF QUESTION PAPER]

ADDITIONAL SPACE FOR ANSWERS

ADDITIONAL SPACE FOR ANSWERS

ADDITIONAL SPACE FOR ANSWERS

[BLANK PAGE]

STANDARD GRADE | GENERAL

2010

[BLANK PAGE]

FOR OFFICIAL USE

G

	KU	RE
Total marks		

2500/403

NATIONAL QUALIFICATIONS 2010	WEDNESDAY, 5 MAY 10.40 AM – 11.15 AM	MATHEMATICS STANDARD GRADE General Level Paper 1 Non-calculator

Fill in these boxes and read what is printed below.

Full name of centre

Town

Forename(s)

Surname

Date of birth

Day	Month	Year	Scottish candidate number	Number of seat

1. **You may not use a calculator.**

2. Answer as many questions as you can.

3. Write your working and answers in the spaces provided. Additional space is provided at the end of this question-answer book for use if required. If you use this space, write clearly the number of the question involved.

4. Full credit will be given only where the solution contains appropriate working.

5. Before leaving the examination room you must give this book to the Invigilator. If you do not, you may lose all the marks for this paper.

FORMULAE LIST

Circumference of a circle: $C = \pi d$

Area of a circle: $A = \pi r^2$

Curved surface area of a cylinder: $A = 2\pi rh$

Volume of a cylinder: $V = \pi r^2 h$

Volume of a triangular prism: $V = Ah$

Theorem of Pythagoras:

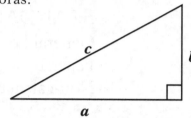

$$a^2 + b^2 = c^2$$

Trigonometric ratios
in a right angled
triangle:

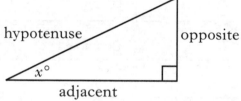

$$\tan x^\circ = \frac{\text{opposite}}{\text{adjacent}}$$

$$\sin x^\circ = \frac{\text{opposite}}{\text{hypotenuse}}$$

$$\cos x^\circ = \frac{\text{adjacent}}{\text{hypotenuse}}$$

Gradient:

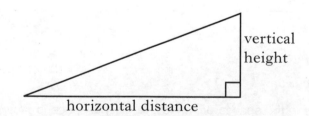

$$\text{Gradient} = \frac{\text{vertical height}}{\text{horizontal distance}}$$

Marks | KU | RE

1. Carry out the following calculations.

(a) $9 \cdot 32 - 5 \cdot 6 + 4 \cdot 27$

1

(b) $37 \cdot 6 \times 8$

1

(c) $2680 \div 400$

1

(d) $7 \times 2\frac{1}{3}$

2

[Turn over

Marks | KU | RE

2. The space shuttle programme costs $5800 million.

Write this number in scientific notation.

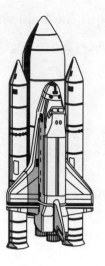

2

3. One day last February, Anna compared the temperature in Edinburgh with the temperature in Montreal.

The temperature in Edinburgh was 8 °C.

The temperature in Montreal was −15 °C.

Find the difference between these temperatures.

2

Marks | KU | RE

4. Complete this design so that the dotted line is an axis of symmetry.

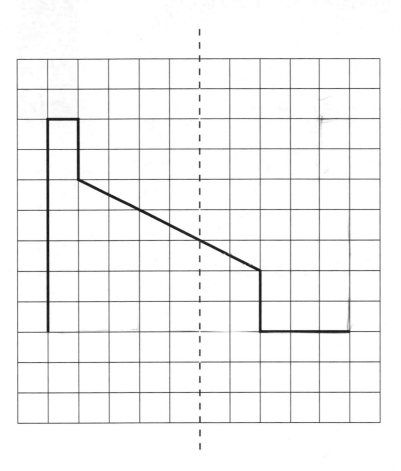

3

[Turn over

DO NOT WRITE IN THIS MARGIN

Marks KU RE

5. Karen asked her class to note the number of songs they downloaded to their phones in the last month.

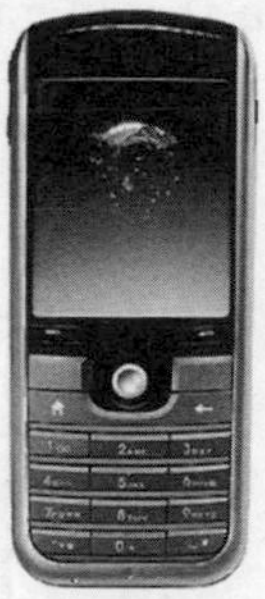

The answers are shown below.

14	16	15	26	11	32	12	13	42	51
27	21	14	17	31	46	33	44	15	17

Display these answers in an ordered stem and leaf diagram.

3

Marks | KU | RE

6. Carla is laying a path in a nursery school.

She is using a mixture of alphabet tiles and coloured tiles.

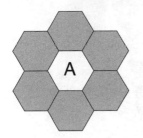

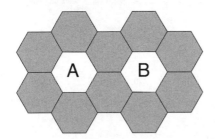

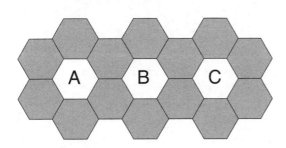

(a) Complete the table below.

Number of alphabet tiles (a)	1	2	3	4	5		12
Number of coloured tiles (c)	6	10					

2

(b) Write down a formula for calculating the number of coloured tiles (c) when you know the number of alphabet tiles (a).

2

(c) Carla uses 86 coloured tiles to make the path.

How many alphabet tiles will be in the path?

2

Marks   KU | RE

7. When on holiday in Spain, Sandy sees a pair of jeans priced at 65 euros.

Sandy knows that he gets 13 euros for £10.

What is the price of the jeans in pounds?

65 euros

3

8. The price of a laptop is reduced from £400 to £320.

Calculate the percentage reduction in the price of the laptop.

£400
£320

3

9. The diagram shows a triangular prism.

The dimensions are given on the diagram.

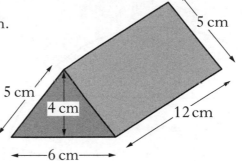

A **net** of this triangular prism is shown below.

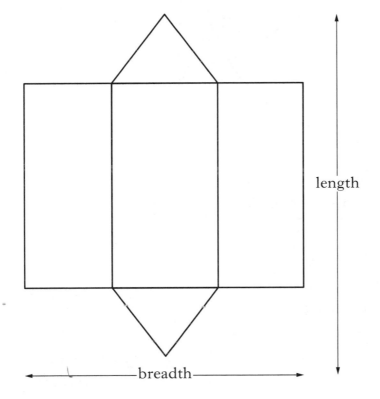

Calculate the length and breadth of this net.

2

[Turn over for Question 10 on *Page ten*

Marks | KU | RE

10.

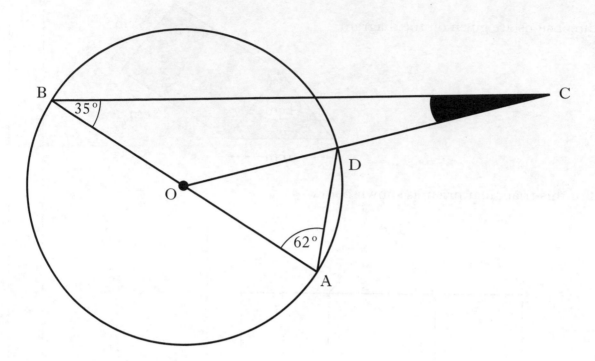

In the diagram above:

- AB is a diameter of the circle with centre O
- OC intersects the circle at D
- Angle ABC = 35°
- Angle BAD = 62°

Calculate the size of the shaded angle.

3

[END OF QUESTION PAPER]

ADDITIONAL SPACE FOR ANSWERS

[BLANK PAGE]

FOR OFFICIAL USE

G

	KU	RE
Total marks		

2500/404

NATIONAL QUALIFICATIONS 2010	WEDNESDAY, 5 MAY 11.35 AM – 12.30 PM	MATHEMATICS STANDARD GRADE General Level Paper 2

Fill in these boxes and read what is printed below.

Full name of centre

Town

Forename(s)

Surname

Date of birth

Day	Month	Year	Scottish candidate number	Number of seat

1. **You may use a calculator.**

2. Answer as many questions as you can.

3. Write your working and answers in the spaces provided. Additional space is provided at the end of this question-answer book for use if required. If you use this space, write clearly the number of the question involved.

4. Full credit will be given only where the solution contains appropriate working.

5. Before leaving the examination room you must give this book to the Invigilator. If you do not, you may lose all the marks for this paper.

FORMULAE LIST

Circumference of a circle: $C = \pi d$

Area of a circle: $A = \pi r^2$

Curved surface area of a cylinder: $A = 2\pi rh$

Volume of a cylinder: $V = \pi r^2 h$

Volume of a triangular prism: $V = Ah$

Theorem of Pythagoras:

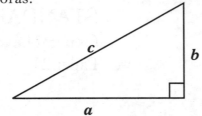

$$a^2 + b^2 = c^2$$

Trigonometric ratios
in a right angled
triangle:

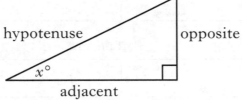

$$\tan x° = \frac{\text{opposite}}{\text{adjacent}}$$

$$\sin x° = \frac{\text{opposite}}{\text{hypotenuse}}$$

$$\cos x° = \frac{\text{adjacent}}{\text{hypotenuse}}$$

Gradient:

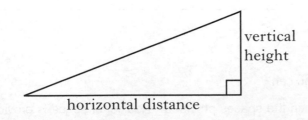

$$\text{Gradient} = \frac{\text{vertical height}}{\text{horizontal distance}}$$

Marks

1. Ten people were asked to guess the number of coffee beans in a jar.

   Their guesses were:

   310 260 198 250 275 300 245 225 310 200

   (a) What is the range of this data?

   1

   (b) Find the median.

   2

   [Turn over

Marks | KU | RE

2. Mr and Mrs Kapela book a cruise to Bruges for themselves and their three children.

- They depart on 27 June

  Mr and Mrs Kapela share an outside cabin and their three children share an inside cabin

  There is a 20% discount for each child

Calculate the total cost of the cruise.

Mini Cruise to Bruges, Belgium		
	Price per person	
Departure Date	Inside Cabin (£)	Outside Cabin (£)
16 May	236	250
30 May	244	274
13 June	266	300
27 June	275	310
12 July	291	325
26 July	312	355
9 Aug	327	370

3

Marks | KU | RE

3. As part of his healthy diet, Tomas has decided to buy fruit in his weekly shopping.

His favourite fruits and their costs per pack are given in the table below.

Fruit	Cost
Apples	£1·25
Oranges	£1·20
Grapes	£2·49
Pears	£1·56
Melon	£1·98

He wants to

- buy 3 different packs of fruit

- spend a maximum of £5 on fruit.

One possible selection and its cost are shown in the table below.

Complete the table to show all of Tomas's possible selections and their cost.

Apples	Oranges	Grapes	Pears	Melon	Cost
✓	✓		✓		£4·01

4

[Turn over

Marks | KU | RE

4. (*a*) Complete the table below for $y = 2x - 3$.

x	−1	1	3
y			

2

(*b*) Using the table in part (*a*), draw the graph of the line $y = 2x - 3$ on the grid below.

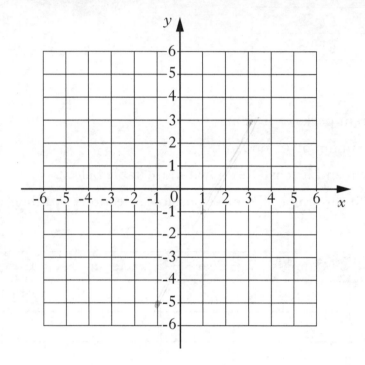

2

Marks | KU | RE

5. For safety reasons the speed limit outside Fairfield Park is 20 miles per hour.

The distance between the speed limit signs outside Fairfield Park is half a mile.

A van took 2 minutes to travel between these signs.

Was the van travelling at a safe speed?

Give a reason for your answer.

3

[Turn over

DO NOT WRITE IN THIS MARGIN

Marks KU RE

6. (*a*) Simplify

$$8(c - 3) + 5(c + 2).$$

3

(*b*) Solve algebraically

$$25 = 7x + 4.$$

2

DO NOT
WRITE IN
THIS
MARGIN

Marks | KU | RE

7. Rowan wants to buy 13 theatre tickets.

The price of one ticket is £12·50.

The theatre has a special online offer of four tickets for the price of three.

Rowan makes use of the special online offer.

How much does Rowan pay for the 13 theatre tickets?

Online Ticket Offer
4 for the price of 3

Theatre

3

[Turn over

Marks KU RE

8. A survey of 1800 first time voters was carried out.
The pie chart below shows how they would vote at the next election.

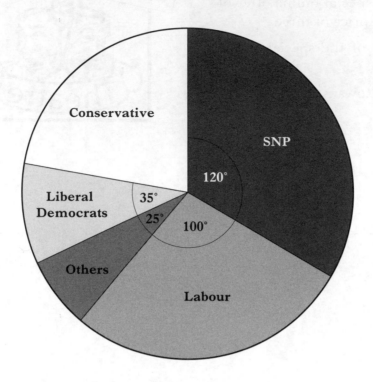

How many of the 1800 first time voters would vote Conservative?

3

Marks | KU | RE

9. A tennis court is 11 metres wide.

It has an area of 264 square metres.

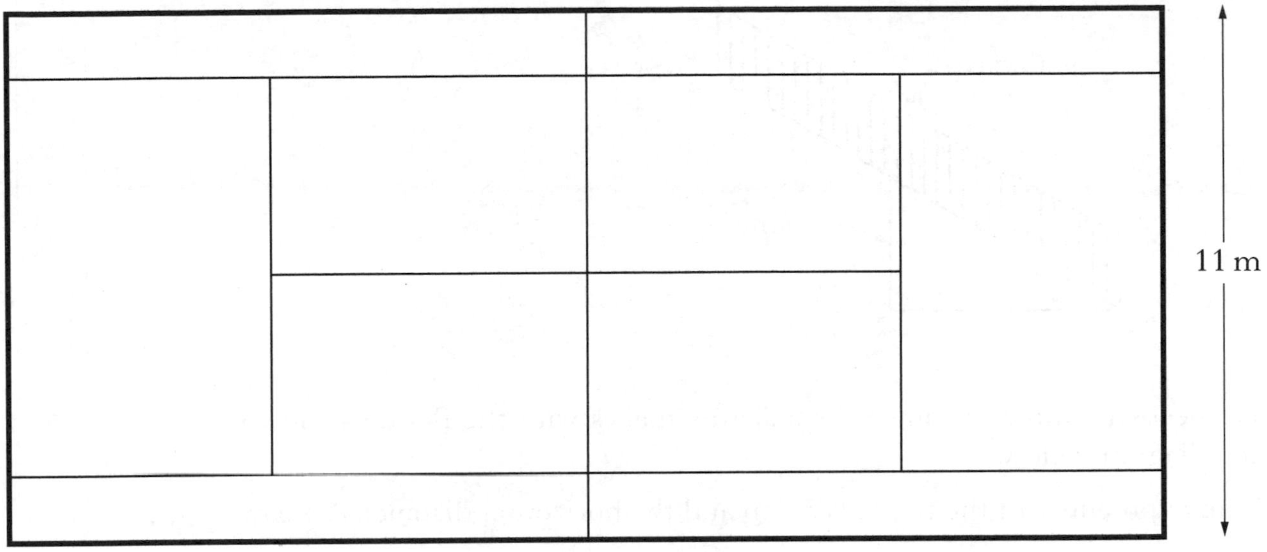

11 m

Calculate the perimeter of the tennis court.

3

[Turn over

Marks | KU | RE

10. Ahmed is making a frame to strengthen a stairway in a shopping centre.

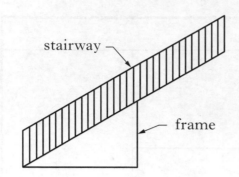

He needs to know the angle the stairway makes with the floor, as shown in the diagram below.

The hypotenuse of the frame is 5·2 m and the horizontal distance is 4·5 m.

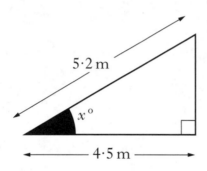

Calculate the size of the shaded angle $x°$.

$$X = \frac{4.5}{5.2}$$

$$X = 0.86$$

$$X = \cos^{-1}(0.86)$$

$$X = 30.1°$$

3

Marks   KU   RE

11.   A climber needs to be rescued.

His position from the helicopter base is marked on the map.

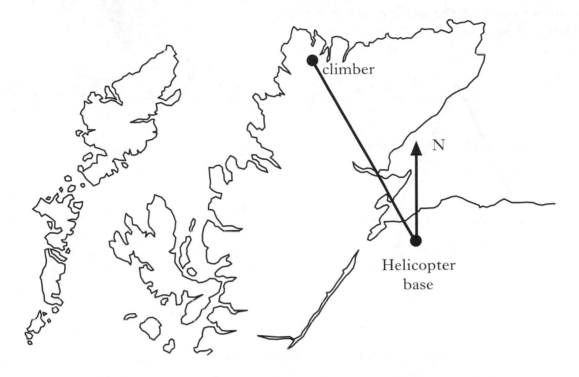

(*a*)   Using a scale of 1 centimetre to 15 kilometres, calculate the distance of the climber from the helicopter base.

1

(*b*)   Find the bearing of the climber from the helicopter base.

2

[Turn over

Marks

12. An earring in the shape of an isosceles triangle is made from silver wire.

The dimensions of the earring are shown on the diagram below.

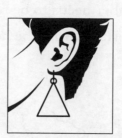

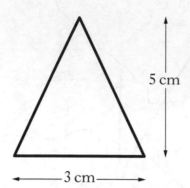

5 cm

←—— 3 cm ——→

Calculate the length of silver wire needed to make a **pair** of earrings.

Do not use a scale drawing.

4

DO NOT
WRITE IN
THIS
MARGIN

Marks

KU | RE

13. A plastic speed bump in the shape of a half cylinder is used to slow traffic outside a Primary School.

The speed bump has radius of 10 centimetres and a length of 7 metres as shown in the diagram below.

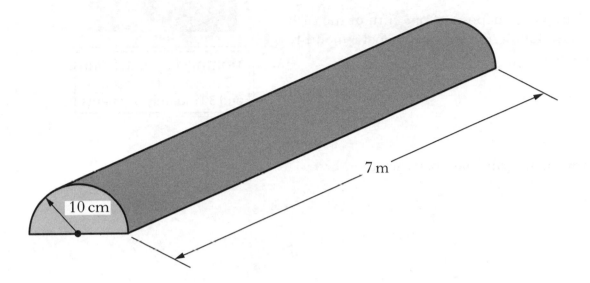

Calculate the volume of plastic used to make the speed bump.

3

[Turn over for Question 14 on *Page sixteen*

Marks   KU   RE

14. Liam buys a new stereo using the monthly payment plan.

The cash price of the stereo is £360.

The total cost of the monthly payment plan is **5% more than the cash price**.

Liam pays a deposit of one fifth of the cash price followed by 30 equal monthly payments.

Cash Price £360

Monthly Payment Plan
Deposit ⅕ of cash price
and 30 monthly payments

How much will Liam pay each month?

4

[END OF QUESTION PAPER]

STANDARD GRADE | GENERAL

2011

[BLANK PAGE]

FOR OFFICIAL USE

G

	KU	RE
Paper 1		
Paper 2		
Total		

2500/403

NATIONAL
QUALIFICATIONS
2011

WEDNESDAY, 4 MAY
10.40 AM – 11.15 AM

MATHEMATICS
STANDARD GRADE
General Level
Paper 1
Non-calculator

Fill in these boxes and read what is printed below.

Full name of centre

Town

Forename(s)

Surname

Date of birth

Day	Month	Year	Scottish candidate number	Number of seat

1. **You may not use a calculator.**

2. Answer as many questions as you can.

3. Write your working and answers in the spaces provided. Additional space is provided at the end of this question-answer book for use if required. If you use this space, write clearly the number of the question involved.

4. Full credit will be given only where the solution contains appropriate working.

5. Before leaving the examination room you must give this book to the Invigilator. If you do not, you may lose all the marks for this paper.

FORMULAE LIST

Circumference of a circle: $C = \pi d$
Area of a circle: $A = \pi r^2$
Curved surface area of a cylinder: $A = 2\pi rh$
Volume of a cylinder: $V = \pi r^2 h$
Volume of a triangular prism: $V = Ah$

Theorem of Pythagoras:

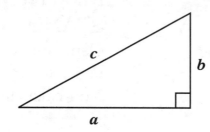

$$a^2 + b^2 = c^2$$

Trigonometric ratios
in a right angled
triangle:

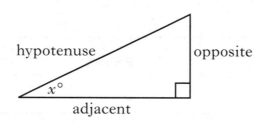

$$\tan x° = \frac{\text{opposite}}{\text{adjacent}}$$

$$\sin x° = \frac{\text{opposite}}{\text{hypotenuse}}$$

$$\cos x° = \frac{\text{adjacent}}{\text{hypotenuse}}$$

Gradient:

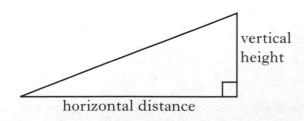

$$\text{Gradient} = \frac{\text{vertical height}}{\text{horizontal distance}}$$

Marks   KU   RE

1. Carry out the following calculations.

(a) $437 \cdot 5 - 95 \cdot 61$

1

(b) $18 \cdot 4 \times 700$

1

(c) $0 \cdot 258 \div 6$

1

(d) Find $\frac{2}{3}$ of 24

2

[Turn over

DO NOT WRITE IN THIS MARGIN

Marks | KU | RE

2. The thickness of a hair on Robbie's head is 0·00254 centimetres. Write 0·00254 in scientific notation.

2.54×10^{3}

2

Marks   KU   RE

3. Margaret is working on the design for a gold bracelet.

She is using gold lengths to make each section.

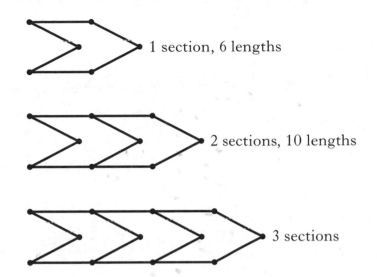

1 section, 6 lengths

2 sections, 10 lengths

3 sections

(a) Complete the table below.

Number of sections (s)	1	2	3	4		10
Number of gold lengths (g)	6	10				

2

(b) Write down a formula for calculating the number of gold lengths, (g), when you know the number of sections (s).

2

(c) Margaret uses 66 gold lengths to make a bracelet.

How many sections does this bracelet contain?

2

[Turn over

DO NOT WRITE IN THIS MARGIN

Marks | KU | RE

4. Sean draws a stem and leaf diagram to display charity donations.

Donation (£)

0	3	5	8			
1	0	0	0	2	2	
2	2	4	8			
3	0	5	5	6	8	8
4	0	0	5			

n = 20 4 | 5 represents £45

Using the above diagram, find:

(*a*) the mode; **1**

(*b*) the median; **2**

(*c*) the range of the donations. **1**

Marks | KU | RE

5. The diagram below shows a large rectangle that has been divided into 3 small rectangles.

The small rectangles are labelled A, B and C.

Some of the dimensions are given on the diagram.

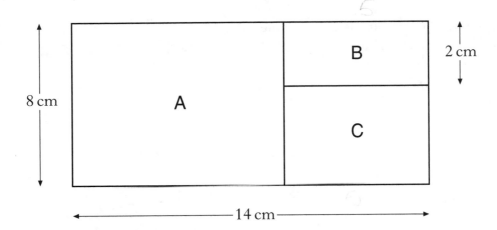

Rectangle B has an area of 10 square centimetres.

Calculate the area of rectangle A.

4

[Turn over

Marks | KU | RE

6. Tom compared the temperatures in the Sahara Desert and at the North Pole.

The temperature in the Sahara Desert was 32 °C.

The temperature at the North Pole was 46 °C less than the temperature in the Sahara Desert.

What was the temperature at the North Pole?

2

7. In the diagram:

- ABCD is a kite

- Angle DAB = 50°

- Angle DBC = 30°

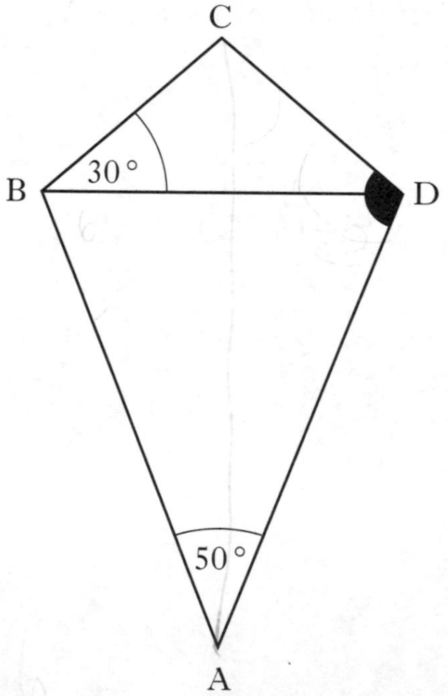

Calculate the size of shaded angle ADC.

3

Marks | KU | RE

8.

Urban Wildlife Park

Admission Charges	
Adult	£13·50
Children aged 3 and under	£10·75
Children aged 4 to 16	£11·50
Family Ticket (1 Adult & 2 Children)	£32·00
Family Ticket (2 Adults & 2 Children)	£42·00
Family Ticket (2 Adults & 3 Children)	£51·00

Alan and Kate take their 12 year old twin daughters to the Urban Wildlife Park.

Instead of buying four individual tickets, they decide to buy a Family Ticket.

How much money do they save?

3

[Turn over for Question 9 on *Page ten*

Marks | KU | RE

9. Three steel nails are shown below.

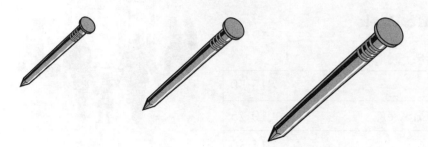

The lengths of the nails are in the ratio 1 : 3 : 5.

The length of the middle nail is 7·5 centimetres.

Calculate the length of the large nail.

3

[END OF QUESTION PAPER]

ADDITIONAL SPACE FOR ANSWERS

[BLANK PAGE]

FOR OFFICIAL USE

G

KU   RE

2500/404

NATIONAL
QUALIFICATIONS
2011

WEDNESDAY, 4 MAY
11.35 AM – 12.30 PM

MATHEMATICS
STANDARD GRADE
General Level
Paper 2

Fill in these boxes and read what is printed below.

Full name of centre

Town

Forename(s)

Surname

Date of birth

Day   Month   Year   Scottish candidate number   Number of seat

1. **You may use a calculator.**

2. Answer as many questions as you can.

3. Write your working and answers in the spaces provided. Additional space is provided at the end of this question-answer book for use if required. If you use this space, write clearly the number of the question involved.

4. Full credit will be given only where the solution contains appropriate working.

5. Before leaving the examination room you must give this book to the Invigilator. If you do not, you may lose all the marks for this paper.

FORMULAE LIST

Circumference of a circle: $C = \pi d$
Area of a circle: $A = \pi r^2$
Curved surface area of a cylinder: $A = 2\pi rh$
Volume of a cylinder: $V = \pi r^2 h$
Volume of a triangular prism: $V = Ah$

Theorem of Pythagoras:

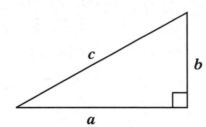

$$a^2 + b^2 = c^2$$

Trigonometric ratios
in a right angled
triangle:

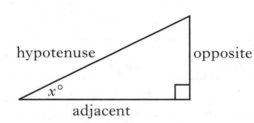

$$\tan x° = \frac{\text{opposite}}{\text{adjacent}}$$

$$\sin x° = \frac{\text{opposite}}{\text{hypotenuse}}$$

$$\cos x° = \frac{\text{adjacent}}{\text{hypotenuse}}$$

Gradient:

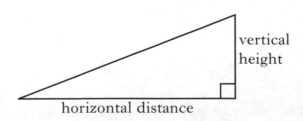

$$\text{Gradient} = \frac{\text{vertical height}}{\text{horizontal distance}}$$

Marks | KU | RE

1. Tariq has a £216 000 mortgage.

The interest rate on this mortgage is 4·5% per annum.

How much does Tariq pay in interest **each month**?

3

[Turn over

Marks

KU | RE

2. There are 2 yellow, 3 red, 1 blue and 4 orange cubes in a bag.

(a) Jason takes a cube from the bag.

What is the probability that it is orange?

1

(b) The cube is replaced in the bag and 3 white cubes are added to the bag.

What is the probability that the next cube taken from the bag is **not** red?

2

DO NOT
WRITE IN
THIS
MARGIN

Marks | KU | RE

3. Andrew is on holiday in Canada and has 600 Canadian Dollars.

He spends 565 Canadian Dollars during his holiday.

At the end of his holiday he changes the remaining Canadian Dollars to Pounds.

The exchange rate is £1 = 1·74 Canadian Dollars.

How much will he receive?

3

[Turn over

Marks | KU | RE

4. For the school gala day the maths teachers have invented a game.

To play the game each person throws **three** bean bags at the target.

Score
8 points for hitting the "Centre" part
5 points for hitting the "Middle" part
2 points for hitting the "Outer" part

All three bean bags must hit the target to win a prize.

Prizes are won for **15 points or more**.

Complete the table below to show all the different ways to win a prize.

Number of bean bags scoring 8 points	Number of bean bags scoring 5 points	Number of bean bags scoring 2 points	Total Points
2	0	1	18

4

Marks | KU | RE

5. Millie and her friends are going hillwalking.

Millie tells her friends that they will start their walk by heading Southwest.

(a) What is the three-figure bearing for Southwest?

1

Later on, Millie tells her friends that they need to walk on a bearing of 135°.

(b) What direction is represented by a bearing of 135°?

1

[Turn over

Marks KU RE

6. (*a*) Factorise fully

$$18 + 12t.$$

2

(*b*) Solve algebraically

$$5m - 3 = 37 + m.$$

3

7. Sally can record and store television programmes using her TV plus system.

The display on her system shows

TVplus
✦ Maximum storage: **80 hours**
✦ Remaining storage: **13%**

- maximum storage space 80 hours

- storage space remaining 13%.

The new TV series of "City Life" has 12 episodes each lasting 55 minutes.

Can she record the whole of the "City Life" series on the remaining storage space?

Give a reason for your answer.

no she mu...

4

[**Turn over**

Marks KU RE

8. Complete this shape so that it has half-turn symmetry about O.

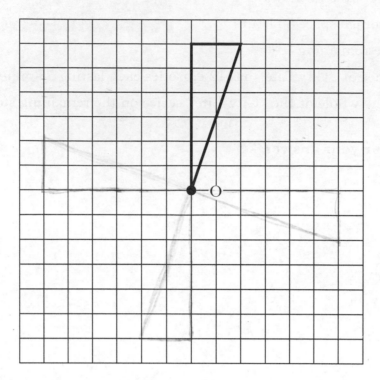

2

9. Larry has invented a device for checking that ladders are positioned at the correct angle.

His design for the device is given below.

Calculate the size of the shaded angle.

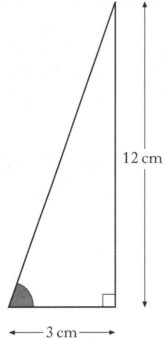

12 cm

3 cm

3

[Turn over

Marks KU RE

10. Vicky makes a number of deliveries in her van.

When the van is moving the on-board computer records the total distance and the average speed.

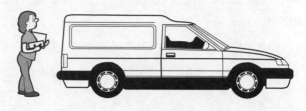

Last Wednesday the computer recorded

- distance = 162 miles

- average speed = 36 miles per hour.

Including stops, Vicky took 6 hours 55 minutes to complete her deliveries.

For how long was Vicky's van stationary?

4

Marks KU RE

11. (*a*) On the grid below, plot the points P (−7, −3) and Q (5, 6).

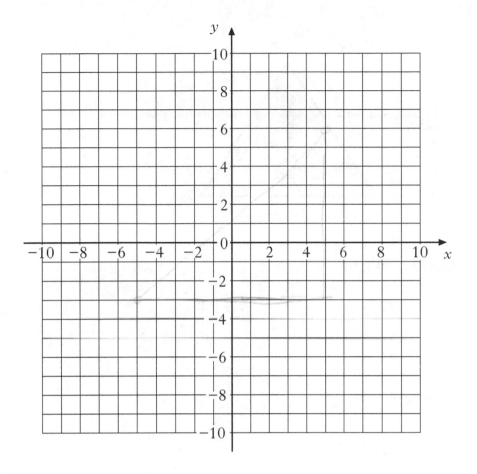

1

(*b*) Find the gradient of line PQ.

2

[Turn over

Marks KU RE

12. A warning sign is in the shape of an isosceles triangle.

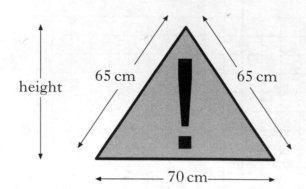

height   65 cm   65 cm

←————70 cm————→

Calculate the height of the sign.

4

DO NOT WRITE IN THIS MARGIN

Marks | KU | RE

13. Helen has recorded the scores for her last eighteen games of golf.

Her scores are shown below.

Score	*Frequency*	*Score × Frequency*
69	3	
70	2	
71	4	
72	4	
73	2	
74	1	
75	2	
	Total = 18	Total =

Complete the above table and find Helen's **mean** score per game.

Round your answer to 1 decimal place.

4

[Turn over for Question 14 on *Page sixteen*

14. Alex uses a circular piece of wood to make a measuring wheel.

The wheel has a radius of 18 centimetres.

How many complete metres are measured by 15 rotations of the wheel?

←18 cm→

4

[END OF QUESTION PAPER]

STANDARD GRADE | ANSWER SECTION

SQA STANDARD GRADE
GENERAL MATHEMATICS 2007–2011

1. (a) 2·438

(b) 261·2

(c) 46·5

(d) $21\frac{2}{3}$

2. 0·000 23 s

3.

Weights	Dance	Running	Cycling	Swimming	Total Time (minutes)
		✓	✓	✓	95
	✓	✓		✓	105
	✓	✓	✓		90
✓	✓			✓	100
✓			✓	✓	90
	✓		✓	✓	115

4.

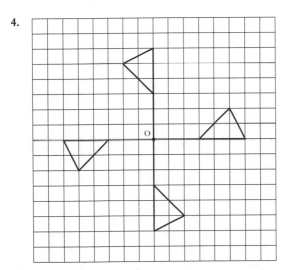

5. 34°

6. (a)

sections	1	2	3	4	5		12
wood	6	11	16	21	26		61

(b) $w = 5s + 1$

(c) $s = 16$

7. (a) and (b)

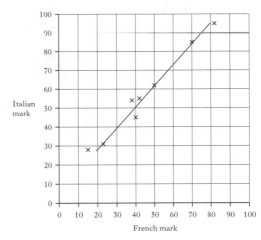

(c) Answer read from line (±2)

8. £61·75

9. (a) $\frac{3}{25}$

(b) $\frac{7}{24}$

10. 320

MATHEMATICS GENERAL
PAPER 2 2007

1. 180 km

2. £4725

3. 3 times per year

4. 188 cm

5. (a) $2x + 26$

   (b) $a \geq 6$

6. 16·06 cm

7. (a) 6·28 m

   (b) Yes, because 40 m is more than 37·7 m

8. £220·50

9. 86°

10. (a) 15 m²

    (b) 52·5 m³

11. 0·4 m

12. (a) 96 min

    (b) 62·5 mm

MATHEMATICS GENERAL
PAPER 1 2008
(NON-CALCULATOR)

1. (a) 14·17

   (b) 57·51

   (c) 0·0437

   (d) 350

2. 4 500 000

3. (a) and (b)

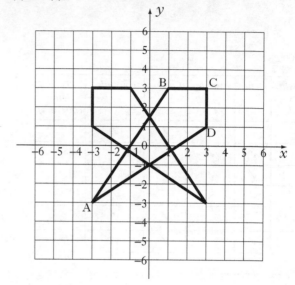

4. $1·04 \times 10^7$

5. (a) 1238, 1247, 1256, 2345

   (b) 2345

6. $-9, -8, 7$

7. £1·22

8. (a) $\frac{2}{3}$

   (b) $\frac{2}{5}$

9. 220°

MATHEMATICS GENERAL PAPER 2 2008

1. £102·55

2. 3 hours 30 minutes

3. (a) 3·575 kg

   (b) 3

4. (a)

Number of M-shapes (m)	1	2	3	4		15
Number of bars (b)	4	7	**10**	**13**		**46**

   (b) $b = 3m + 1$

   (c) 25

5. 17 cm

6. 40%

7.

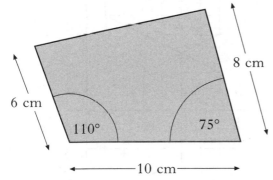

8. (a) $t = 8$

   (b) $4(5x - 3y)$

9. 7·326 m

10.

Parking time (hours)	Frequency	Parking time × frequency
1	28	28
2	22	44
3	10	30
4	15	60
5	11	55
6	5	30
7	9	63
	Total = 100	Total = 310

   Mean parking time = 3·1 hours

11. 77

12. 24·4°

13. (a) 399 000 cm³

    (b) 131·9 cm

MATHEMATICS GENERAL PAPER 1 2009 (NON-CALCULATOR)

1. (a) 2·44

   (b) 138 000

   (c) 36·7

   (d) 43·2

2. $2·96 \times 10^{-2}$

3. (a)

Number of sections (s)	1	2	3	4	5		11
Number of metal rings (r)	4	9	**14**	**19**	**24**		**54**

   (b) $r = 5s - 1$

   (c) 16

4.

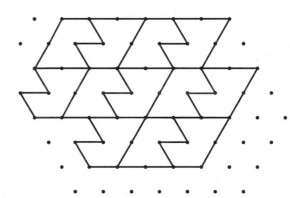

5. (a), (b), (c)

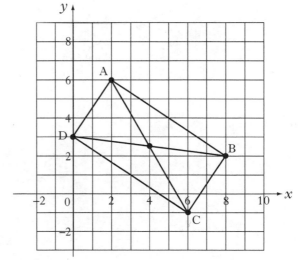

6. −17°C

7. 200 grams

8. (a)

```
5    3    3    4    6    8
6    1    2    3    5    7    8
7    0    4    6    6
8    3    4    5    8
                        n = 19    5|3 = 5·3
```

   (b) 6·7 cm

9. 143°

MATHEMATICS GENERAL
PAPER 2 2009

1. 42 mph

2. £56·80

3. 641 cm²

4. (a) 2h 15 min

   (b) 2255

5. (a) 3(2c − 5d)

   (b) a + 15

6. (a)

Selections				Cost
Drama	Sport	Movies	Music	52
Drama	Sport	Movies	Kids	54
Drama	Sport	Kids	Music	49
Drama	Movies	Kids	Music	44
Sport	Movies	Kids	Music	57

   (b) Sport, Movies, Kids, Music (£57)

7. 3·3 hrs

8. 3·4 m

9. £22·25

10. £74·40

11. 8·45

12. Yes, 3m³ left over

13.

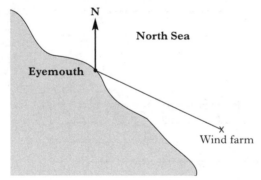

14. 5 cm

MATHEMATICS GENERAL
PAPER 1 2010
(NON-CALCULATOR)

1. (a) 7·99

   (b) 300·8

   (c) 6·7

   (d) $16\frac{1}{3}$

2. $5·8 \times 10^9$

3. 23°C

4.

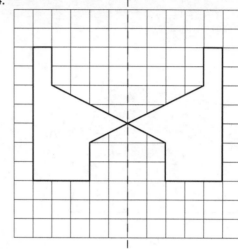

5. 1 | 1 2 3 4 4 5 5 6 7 7
   2 | 1 6 7
   3 | 1 2 3
   4 | 2 4 6
   5 | 1

6. (a)

Number of alphabet tiles (a)	1	2	3	4	5		12
Number of coloured tiles (c)	6	10	14	18	22		50

   (b) c = 4a + 2

   (c) 21

7. £50

8. 20%

9. 1 = 20   b = 16

10. 21°

MATHEMATICS GENERAL
PAPER 2 2010

1. (a) 112

(b) 255

2. £1280

3.

Apples	Oranges	Grapes	Pears	Melon	Cost
✓	✓		✓		£4·01
✓	✓	✓			£4·94
✓	✓			✓	£4·43
✓			✓	✓	£4·79
	✓		✓	✓	£4·74

4. (a) −5, −1, 3

(b)

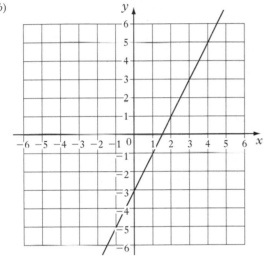

5. Yes, speed only 15 mph

6. (a) $13c - 14$

(b) $x = 3$

7. £125

8. 400

9. 70 m

10. 30·1°

11. (a) 82·5 km

(b) 330 (± 2)°

12. 26·8 cm

13. 109900 cm³

14. £10·20

MATHEMATICS GENERAL
PAPER 1 2011
(NON-CALCULATOR)

1. (a) 341·89

(b) 12880

(c) 0·043

(d) 16

2. $2·54 \times 10^{-3}$

3. (a)

1	2	3	4		10
6	10	14	18		42

(b) $g = 4s + 2$

(c) 16

4. (a) 10

(b) 26

(c) 42

5. 72 cm²

6. −14°C

7. 95°

8. £8

9. 12·5 cm

MATHEMATICS GENERAL
PAPER 2 2011

1. £810

2. (a) 4/10 or equivalent

   (b) 10/13 or equivalent

3. £20·11

4.

8 points	5 points	2 points	Total
2	0	1	18
3	0	0	24
2	1	0	21
1	2	0	18
1	1	1	15
0	3	0	15

5. (a) 225°

   (b) Southeast

6. (a) $6(3 + 2t)$

   (b) $m = 10$

7. No, only 10·4 hours available and 11 hours required

8.

9. 75·96

10. 2 hours 25 minutes

11. (a)

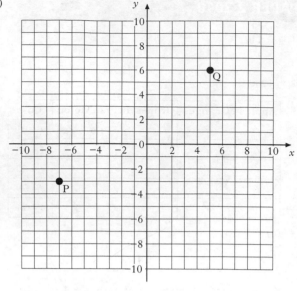

   (b) 9/12

12. 54·8 cm

13. 71·6

14. 16 (complete metres)

Hey! I've done it

iBrightRED
PUBLISHING

Published by Bright Red Publishing Ltd, 6 Stafford Street, Edinburgh, EH3 7AU
Tel: 0131 220 5804, Fax: 0131 220 6710, enquiries: sales@brightredpublishing.co.uk,
www.brightredpublishing.co.uk

Official SQA answers to 978-1-84948-176-2
2007-2011